Put Beginning Readers on the Right Track with
ALL ABOARD READING™

The All Aboard Reading series is especially designed for beginning readers. Written by noted authors and illustrated in full color, these are books that children really want to read—books to excite their imagination, expand their interests, make them laugh, and support their feelings. With fiction and nonfiction stories that are high interest and curriculum-related, All Aboard Reading books offer something for every young reader. And with four different reading levels, the All Aboard Reading series lets you choose which books are most appropriate for your children and their growing abilities.

Picture Readers
Picture Readers have super-simple texts, with many nouns appearing as rebus pictures. At the end of each book are 24 flash cards—on one side is a rebus picture; on the other side is the written-out word.

Station Stop 1
Station Stop 1 books are best for children who have just begun to read. Simple words and big type make these early reading experiences more comfortable. Picture clues help children to figure out the words on the page. Lots of repetition throughout the text helps children to predict the next word or phrase—an essential step in developing word recognition.

Station Stop 2
Station Stop 2 books are written specifically for children who are reading with help. Short sentences make it easier for early readers to understand what they are reading. Simple plots and simple dialogue help children with reading comprehension.

Station Stop 3
Station Stop 3 books are perfect for children who are reading alone. With longer text and harder words, these books appeal to children who have mastered basic reading skills. More complex stories captivate children who are ready for more challenging books.

In addition to All Aboard Reading books, look for All Aboard Math Readers™ (fiction stories that teach math concepts children are learning in school); All Aboard Science Readers™ (nonfiction books that explore the most fascinating science topics in age-appropriate language); All Aboard Poetry Readers™ (funny, rhyming poems for readers of all levels); and All Aboard Mystery Readers™ (puzzling tales where children piece together evidence with the characters).

All Aboard for happy reading!

For my husband, Dan, and our daughter, Clara Rose.
You light up my life!—M.E.B.

To Linda, for her grace and courage.—C.S.

GROSSET & DUNLAP
Published by the Penguin Group
Penguin Group (USA) Inc., 375 Hudson Street, New York, New York 10014, USA
Penguin Group (Canada), 90 Eglinton Avenue East, Suite 700, Toronto,
Ontario M4P 2Y3, Canada (a division of Pearson Penguin Canada Inc.)
Penguin Books Ltd., 80 Strand, London WC2R 0RL, England
Penguin Group Ireland, 25 St. Stephen's Green, Dublin 2, Ireland
(a division of Penguin Books Ltd.)
Penguin Group (Australia), 250 Camberwell Road, Camberwell, Victoria 3124,
Australia (a division of Pearson Australia Group Pty. Ltd.)
Penguin Books India Pvt. Ltd., 11 Community Centre, Panchsheel Park,
New Delhi—110 017, India
Penguin Group (NZ), 67 Apollo Drive, Rosedale, North Shore 0632, New Zealand
(a division of Pearson New Zealand Ltd.)
Penguin Books (South Africa) (Pty.) Ltd., 24 Sturdee Avenue,
Rosebank, Johannesburg 2196, South Africa

Penguin Books Ltd., Registered Offices:
80 Strand, London WC2R 0RL, England

Text copyright © 2008 by Megan E. Bryant. Illustrations copyright © 2008 by Carol Schwartz. All rights reserved. Published by Grosset & Dunlap, a division of Penguin Young Readers Group, 345 Hudson Street, New York, New York 10014. ALL ABOARD SCIENCE READER and GROSSET & DUNLAP are trademarks of Penguin Group (USA) Inc. Printed in the U.S.A.

Library of Congress Cataloging-in-Publication Data

Bryant, Megan E.
Fireflies / by Megan E. Bryant ; illustrated by Carol Schwartz.
p. cm.
ISBN-13: 978-0-448-44834-3 (pbk.)
1. Fireflies--Juvenile literature. I. Schwartz, Carol, 1954- ill. II. Title.
QL596.L28B79 2008
595.76'44--dc22
2007043365

ISBN 978-0-448-44834-3   10 9 8 7 6 5 4 3 2

Fireflies

By Megan E. Bryant
Illustrated by Carol Schwartz

Grosset & Dunlap

It is the end of a warm

summer day.

The sun is setting.

In the twilight, something flashes.

Over there.

Over here.

And over there again!

Look!

The sky is filled with fireflies!

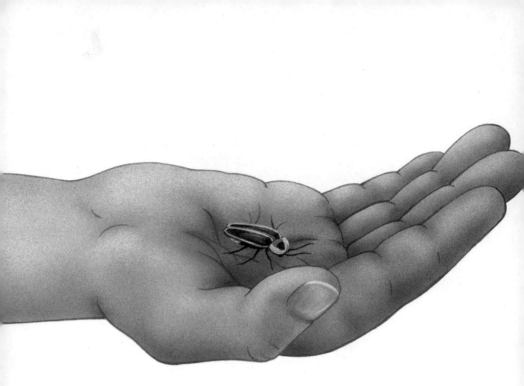

Have you ever looked for fireflies

on a summer night?

If so, you're not alone!

For thousands of years,

people all over the world

have been fascinated by fireflies.

Long ago in China, people thought

fireflies burst from burning grass.

People in Europe thought
they were fairies.
Native Americans used fireflies
to make glowing face paint.
But what are fireflies?
And what makes them glow?

Fireflies aren't really flies at all.

They are actually beetles!

Like all beetles, a firefly has

two pairs of wings.

It has six legs and two antennae.

And it has a body that is split

into three parts—the head, the thorax,

and the abdomen.

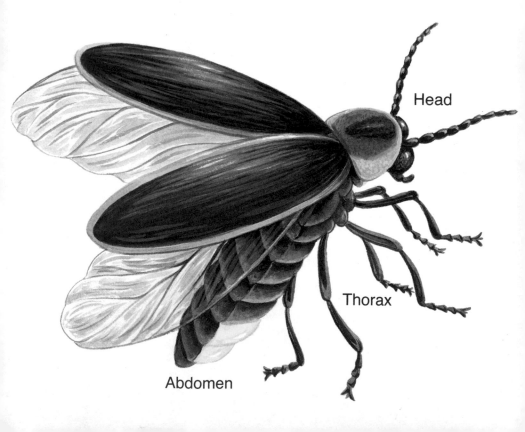

Head

Thorax

Abdomen

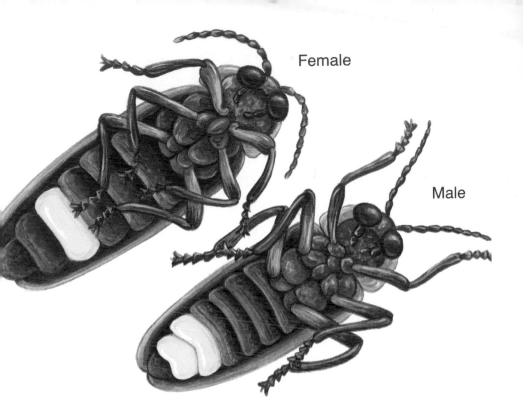

Female

Male

The end of the abdomen

is the part that lights up!

Male fireflies glow more brightly

than female fireflies.

That's because a male firefly's abdomen

has two sections that light up.

A female firefly's abdomen

has only one light-up section.

In the United States, there are about 170 different species of fireflies. And there are about 2,000 kinds of fireflies around the world!

Scientists think there are
even more species of fireflies
that have not been discovered yet.
Most fireflies live in Asia, South
America, and Central America.
Some Asian fireflies have gills,
like fish.
They live underwater!

Most fireflies like to live
in warm, wet places.
You can find lots of them
in jungles, marshes, and swamps.
They also like to live in fields
of tall grass.

In the United States, fireflies live in places with hot, humid summer weather—like the South and the Northeast.

How do fireflies light up?

For many years, no one knew.

Then scientists discovered that

fireflies have genes that make two

special glow chemicals.

The glow chemicals mix with

another chemical in the firefly's

body called ATP.

ATP is found in all living
things—even you!
When a little oxygen from the
firefly's cells is added to the mix,
it makes a flash of light!

The main reason fireflies light up

is to find a mate.

Each firefly species flashes its light

in a special pattern.

And each firefly's flash pattern

is slightly different.

If one firefly likes another
firefly's flash pattern,
they will mate.

Fireflies usually try to avoid other species of fireflies.

Fireflies from the same species fly at the same height.

Some species fly just a few feet off the ground,

while others fly high in the trees.

That way, they won't get confused

by another species's flash pattern—

and try to mate with the wrong kind

of firefly.

But not all flashes are used
to attract mates.

Some female fireflies use their
flashes to trap prey.

They copy another kind of
firefly's flash.

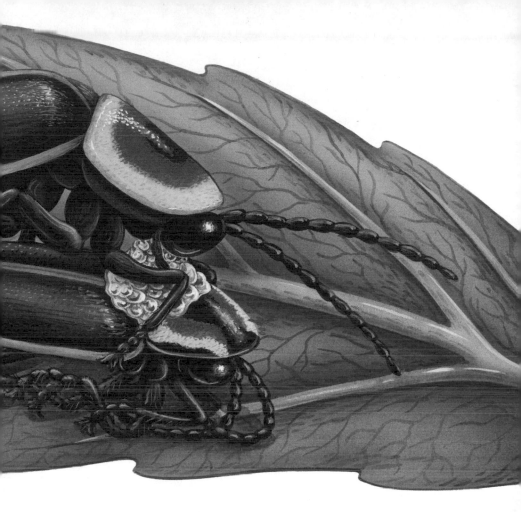

A male firefly from another species

thinks that he has found a mate.

But when he comes close,

the female firefly attacks!

Now she has a tasty meal.

There might be dozens,

or even hundreds,

of fireflies in the same field.

Each one will flash separately.

But sometimes in Asia, and in a few

places in the United States,

hundreds of fireflies will start

flashing together!

They will all flash in exactly

the same pattern,

at exactly the same time.

This is so rare that scientists

don't know how fireflies

do it—or why.

But it is an amazing sight to see.

Most fireflies sleep all day.

At dusk, the fireflies awake.

The male firefly climbs a piece of grass.

He flies straight up into the air.

Then he starts flashing his light.

Nearby, a female firefly waits on a leaf.

If she likes the male firefly's light,

she will flash back.

Sometimes the fireflies flash

back and forth for over an hour!

If they like each other,

the two fireflies will mate.

A few days after the fireflies mate,
the female lays 500 to 1,000 eggs.
The eggs glow softly
in the damp dirt.

After two to four weeks,

the eggs hatch.

Out crawl the baby fireflies.

They are called larvae.

They have soft, brown bodies.

And they can glow!

That is how the larvae tell predators

that they taste bad.

Firefly larvae live underground,

on rotting wood, or under

fallen leaves.

They eat and grow,

and eat and grow some more.

Most adult fireflies don't eat anything,

so the larvae need to fill up now!

Firefly larvae love to eat slugs,
worms, and snails.

This larva is hunting some prey.

It follows a slug's slime trail.

Then it bites the slug and injects

it with a chemical to paralyze it.

The chemical also turns

the slug's guts to goo!

Then the larva sucks out

the guts—leaving just the slug's

empty body behind.

Gross!

During winter, the firefly larvae

burrow underground.

In the spring, they come out

to eat some more.

After one or two years,

the larvae are ready to become adults.

Each larva builds a house
underground.

The little mud house is only

the size of a marble,

but it's just right for the larva.

Inside the mud house,
something amazing happens.
In about ten to twenty days,
the larva transforms into an
adult firefly!

It comes out of the house

and starts flashing right away.

It will only live as an adult firefly

for a few weeks.

All it wants to do is find a mate

so that the firefly life cycle

can continue.

But fireflies aren't just fun to watch.

Not long ago, scientists wondered

if the firefly's glow could help them

in their research.

First, they had to figure out if

the firefly chemicals would glow

in another living thing.

They put firefly genes
into some tobacco plants.
When the plants started glowing,
the scientists knew that their
experiment had worked!

Now fireflies are helping

to cure diseases.

Scientists put firefly genes

into cancer cells.

When the glowing cancer cell moves,

scientists track it to learn

how cancer spreads.

And when the cell stops glowing,

it means that the cancer cell has died.

Someday, firefly genes
may help to cure cancer.
Scientists are working on a
treatment that makes cancer cells
very sensitive to light.

Then they add the firefly genes
to the cancer cells.
That makes the cancer cells
light up—and then they self-destruct!

Fireflies might even help us

find out if there are other living

beings in outer space!

Special sensors, filled with

firefly chemicals,

are being made by scientists.

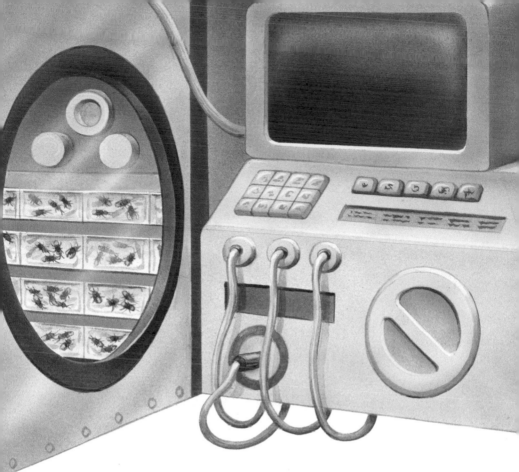

When the sensors are fully built,

they will be launched on space missions.

If they start glowing, it means

there is ATP nearby.

And since ATP is in all living things,

astronauts will know if there

is life in space!

But fireflies need our help.

Every year, there are fewer

and fewer fireflies.

Fireflies were once so valuable

to scientists that "firefly hunters"

would catch them by the thousands.

Luckily, scientists can now make

firefly chemicals and genes in the lab.

But firefly hunters had already caught

too many fireflies.

Construction is wrecking the fields,

marshes, and woods where fireflies live.

Bright outdoor lights make it hard

for fireflies to see one another's flashes.

And bug spray used to kill mosquitoes

hurts fireflies, too.

You can help fireflies
by making your yard firefly-friendly.
At night, turn off outdoor lights
and any bright lights inside
your house.
Don't use bug spray outside.

Tall grass, low tree branches,
and bushes in your yard
will give fireflies a place to live.
If you catch fireflies in a jar or
paper bag, always set them free
before bedtime.

Fireflies are a special part
of summer nights.
If we protect them,
we can enjoy their lights—
and learn their other secrets, too!